CUBAN MISSILE CRISIS

A Life From Beginning to End

Copyright © 2018 by Hourly History.

All rights reserved.

Table of Contents

Introduction
World War to Cold War
Mutually Assured Destruction
Revolution in Cuba
The Missile Gap
American Build-up and Provocation
Russian Missiles Arrive in Cuba
Escalation
Kennedy Speaks to America
On the Edge of the Abyss
The Blink
Conclusion

Introduction

What became known as the Cold War between the United States of America and the Soviet Union lasted from just after the end of World War II in 1945 until 1991. It was a covert war, fought mainly using spies and subterfuge, but occasionally involving armed conflict by proxy as combatants armed and supported by one superpower or the other fought each other in various parts of the world.

The main reason that the tension between the superpowers never developed into outright war was simple: by the late 1940s, both Russia and America had nuclear weapons. Within ten years, both had sufficient nuclear weapons to destroy the other completely. Neither could afford to start a war which might lead to a nuclear exchange. The resulting situation was extremely dangerous and relied on a delicate balance to keep the peace. If one side gained a distinct advantage in the struggle for nuclear supremacy, it might believe that a nuclear war was winnable and therefore acceptable.

In the 50 years of the Cold War, there were times when tension between the two superpowers became almost unbearable. Only once, however, did an all-out nuclear war look not only possible but likely. For two weeks in October of 1962, the whole world watched in horror as a confrontation between the United States and the Soviet Union regarding the island of Cuba escalated to the point that armed and nuclear conflict between the two seemed inevitable. It isn't over-dramatic to say that such a war would almost certainly have meant the end of the civilized world and perhaps even the end of life on earth.

This the story of how the Cuban Missile Crisis came about and how, at the very last moment, nuclear war was avoided.

Chapter One
World War to Cold War

"An iron curtain has descended across the Continent."

—Winston Churchill, March 1946

During World War II, the United States of America and the Soviet Union were allies. But once the Nazis and the Japanese were defeated in 1945, the two superpowers became increasingly distrustful of each other. America believed that Russia planned to spread communism across the world. Russia believed that America was inherently anti-communist and wanted to see all parts of the world converted to capitalism. This mutual distrust was the basis for a covert, undeclared war between the two most powerful nations on earth that lasted for more than 40 years.

Part of the reason for the hostility between Russia and America was philosophical. Capitalism and communism are diametrically opposed in terms of ideology: Communism stresses collective responsibility, ownership, accountability, and reward under an unelected and powerful leadership. Capitalism, on the other hand, is focused on individual freedom, initiative, and reward supported by the democratic process. This ideological difference led to distrust between the superpowers and an almost evangelical zeal for each to spread its own doctrine to other parts of the world.

After the end of World War II, Russia—under the absolute control of Joseph Stalin, the Secretary of the Central Committee of the Communist Party—attempted to introduce communist regimes in a number of countries around the world, either by direct military intervention or by supplying communist insurgencies with weapons and support. A series of American presidents attempted to block the spread of communism by providing economic and military aid to regimes they saw as friendly, and by backing this up with the threat of military intervention.

The other reason for tension between Russia and America was a substantial difference in the experience of each country during World War II. America lost around 400,000 people during the war, and no American city was damaged as a result of fighting or bombing. The United States emerged from World War II with its cities and industry intact and with the most powerful economy in the world. Russia, however, lost about 24 million people, and most of its largest cities, industrial centers, and infrastructure were destroyed during the four years of fighting. Following the end of the war, the Soviet Union was forced to spend vast sums on reconstruction and rebuilding all that had been destroyed by the German invasion.

The result was that Stalin and the leaders of the Soviet Union believed, not without reason, that Russia had borne the brunt of fighting against Nazi Germany. They felt that Russia was therefore due more of the spoils of war, particularly in Europe. America was concerned at the prospect of a Russian-controlled Europe and tried to block the spread of Russian power in mainland Europe. The outcome was a Europe split into east and west and divided by a border which quickly became known as the Iron Curtain, the divide between the communist-controlled east and the American-dominated west.

Following the end of the war, Germany was divided into two separate countries: The Federal Republic of Germany (often known as West Germany) was within the American sphere of influence while the German Democratic Republic (often known as East Germany) was within the Soviet zone. By the mid-1950s, West Germany had joined the United Kingdom, France, Belgium, Portugal, Denmark, Italy, Austria, and other countries in the American-dominated North Atlantic Treaty Organization (NATO) while East Germany joined Poland, Czechoslovakia, Romania, Hungary, and Yugoslavia to become part of the Russian-dominated Warsaw Pact. It rapidly became clear to both sides that neither could expect to gain more territory in Europe without risking a major war. For this reason, both Russia and America began to look at other areas of the world to expand their respective ideologies.

In 1949, the communists made a huge gain when China, one of the largest and most populous countries in the world, came under the control of Mao Zedong and reinvented itself as the Communist People's Republic of China. Other countries in South East Asia seemed set to follow with large communist insurgencies in Korea and

Vietnam and smaller uprisings in countries such as Malaya and Thailand. In 1949, America and other NATO countries found themselves drawn into open war against communist forces in North Korea backed by the People's Republic of China. Later, America would become involved in an unsuccessful war in Vietnam against communist forces backed and supported by Russia.

Although the period following World War II saw many armed conflicts between groups supported by Russia and America, there was no fighting directly between the two superpowers. Instead of overt military confrontation, the two conflicting ideologies fought by proxy through the support of various warring factions. The main reason that both the United States and the Soviet Union sought to avoid armed conflict with each other was the existence of a devastating new weapon which had emerged during World War II: the nuclear bomb.

Chapter Two

Mutually Assured Destruction

"Every man, woman and child lives under a nuclear sword of Damocles, hanging by the slenderest of threads, capable of being cut at any moment by accident or miscalculation or by madness."

—President John F. Kennedy

In 1939, American President Franklin D. Roosevelt authorized the first research on the use of nuclear materials to make weapons. He did this because of reports from American intelligence agencies that Nazi scientists were working on a similar project. This intelligence proved to be misleading; although Nazi scientists were looking at various potential uses of uranium, there never was a concerted attempt to build a Nazi atomic weapon. Initially, U.S. research on the development of a nuclear weapon was limited to providing funding to allow two notable physicists, Enrico Fermi and Leo Szilard, to research at Columbia University.

When America joined World War II after the Japanese attack on Pearl Harbor in December 1941, the development of a nuclear weapon became more urgent, and by December 1942, the Manhattan Project had been created with the express object of producing a weapon which used nuclear energy. In 1943, renowned physicist Dr. Robert Oppenheimer was appointed director of the main site of Project Manhattan at Los Alamos in New Mexico.

At 05:30 am on July 16, 1945, in a part of the New Mexico desert which formed the USAAF Alamogordo Bombing and Gunnery Range, the first nuclear weapon was detonated. Up to that point, none of the scientists working on the project had been completely certain that the bomb would actually detonate; some predicted that it would fizzle rather than explode. As it would turn out, the very first nuclear bomb exploded with a force equivalent to twenty kilotons of TNT, produced a shock wave which was felt more than one hundred miles away, raised a mushroom cloud seven miles high, and melted the desert sand into glass. The age of nuclear weapons had arrived.

The engineers and scientists who had created the test weapon had also built two nuclear bombs capable of being dropped from aircraft: the uranium-based "Little Boy" and the plutonium-based "Fat Man." Although Nazi Germany had surrendered in May 1945, Japan was still fighting, and on June 26 at the Potsdam Conference, the Japanese were called upon to surrender or to face "prompt and utter destruction." On August 6, 1945, Little Boy was dropped on the Japanese city of Hiroshima. Three days later, on August 9, Fat Man was dropped on Nagasaki. The following day, August 10, 1945, the Japanese announced their intention to surrender. World War II was over.

In the years immediately following the end of the war, America was the only country in the world to possess the technology to make nuclear weapons. This made the U.S. the most powerful nation in the world, and almost immediately, the Soviet Union accelerated work on developing their own nuclear weapons. This work progressed far more rapidly than anyone expected, partly due to the Soviet acquisition of German nuclear scientists following World War II and assisted by the theft of secret information from the American nuclear project by Russian spies. On August 29, 1949, the first Russian nuclear weapon was tested successfully in Kazakhstan.

In the years that followed, a nuclear arms race developed between the United States and the Soviet Union with both attempting to produce larger numbers of more powerful nuclear bombs than the other. In 1952, the U.S. tested the first prototype of an even more powerful nuclear weapon: the hydrogen bomb. This weapon was 2,500 times more powerful than the bomb dropped on Hiroshima. In 1953, Russia also detonated a hydrogen bomb.

Initially, nuclear weapons were bombs designed to be carried by long-range strategic bombers. Such bombers, however, could be shot down before they reached their targets, and both Russia and America devoted a great deal of time and money to develop more effective and reliable means of delivering nuclear weapons. Both powers used technology from the emerging space-race to create missiles which could carry nuclear warheads. By the late 1950s, these Inter-Continental Ballistic Missiles (ICBMs) could deliver a nuclear warhead anywhere in the world. By 1961, there were estimated to be enough nuclear warheads to destroy the entire surface of the planet and sufficient ICBMs to deliver them precisely and reliably.

The sheer power of hydrogen bombs delivered by missiles changed the face of warfare. Studies in the United States in the late 1950s suggested that an all-out Russian nuclear attack might kill anywhere from 20 to 90 million Americans and leave many times that number injured or ill. Combined with the inevitable destruction of American cities, industrial capacity, and infrastructure, it was obvious that the U.S. could not emerge from any nuclear exchange with the Soviet Union as a world superpower. Studies in Russia concluded precisely the same thing.

First-strike missiles launched from either Russia or America would take somewhere around 30 minutes to cross the North Pole and reach their targets. This would give the other side sufficient time to detect the incoming missiles and launch a retaliatory second strike. Neither side could therefore afford to launch a nuclear strike on the other because they knew that the reply would be just as devastating. A nuclear war between Russia and America would not allow either to gain world supremacy—it would instead reduce both countries to radioactive wastelands. This knowledge that neither side could afford to launch a nuclear strike on the other without invoking its own demise became known as Mutually Assured Destruction (MAD).

MAD was indeed a deterrent which prevented either side from attacking the other, but it had a major flaw: if either side could develop some means of delivering their first-strike nuclear attack quicker, they might be able to destroy the other's capacity to mount a counter-strike (this is sometimes referred to as a decapitation strike). MAD relied on balance; if this balance was disturbed, one side or the other might believe that they could deliver a nuclear knock-out blow to the other without risking a catastrophic retaliation.

Chapter Three
Revolution in Cuba

"I think the big tragedy of the Cuban Revolution was that it became dependent on the Soviet Union."

—Tariq Ali, journalist and political activist

Most of the countries which fell to communist revolution or insurgency in the period following World War II were physically distant from America. The increase of Russian influence in countries like China and the northern part of Korea were troubling, but they did not pose a direct military threat to the American mainland. However, rebels had been fighting a guerrilla war since 1954 in a country much closer to America and which potentially posed a direct threat to the security of the United States.

The island of Cuba in the Caribbean was ruled by Spain following the arrival of Christopher Columbus in the late fifteenth century until the Spanish-American War of the late nineteenth century when Cuba was occupied by American troops. In 1902, Cuba—which is located just 100 miles from the southern tip of Florida—became nominally independent, but its economy relied heavily on American investments and business interests.

In 1933, a young sergeant in the Cuban army named Fulgencio Batista y Zaldívar led a revolt against the provisional government. Batista appointed himself leader of the Cuban Armed Forces and effectively ruled the country by leading the five-man group that took the place of the elected government. When an election was held in 1940 to appoint a new president, Batista won and was appointed the ninth president of Cuba. He ruled for a four-year term, after which he moved to Florida in the United States.

In 1952, Batista returned to Cuba to run for president again. When it became apparent that he stood no chance of election against more left-wing candidates, he staged another coup and established himself as leader. His presidency was recognized by America less than two weeks after the coup. The United States was concerned about the potential spread of communism in the Caribbean and saw the right-wing Batista as a useful ally in the region.

When Batista became president for the second time, Cuba was one of the most prosperous Caribbean countries, but the new president soon changed that. The Batista regime was characterized by extreme corruption and graft. The American Mafia virtually ran the lucrative casino business in Cuba, and Batista sold business interests to a large number of American companies—by the late 1950s, American companies owned 90% of all Cuban mines, 80% of public utility companies, and 40% of the sugar business. Profits from these companies went back to the United States or were distributed amongst corrupt officials in the Cuban government.

Poverty and unrest in Cuba increased, and Batista responded with increasing brutality; arbitrary arrests, torture, and public executions were used to repress any opposition to his regime. Many people in the United States were concerned about supporting such a violent dictator; when he was running for the presidency in 1960, Senator John F. Kennedy referred to Batista's rule in Cuba as a "reign of terror."

In response, two brothers, Fidel and Raul Castro, began an armed insurrection against Batista in 1953. In 1956, they and a group of armed rebels arrived in Cuba and escaped into the inaccessible Sierra Maestra Mountains. From there, they expanded the size of their rebel army, and in August 1958, they began an offensive against the armed forces of Batista's government. By January 1, 1959, Batista had fled to the Dominican Republic, and by January 3, a president appointed by Castro was in control of Cuba.

Although Castro was not overtly communist at first (in fact, he vehemently denied being a communist when he first came to power), it was clear that he favored the sort of collective ownership of resources and property that characterized many communist countries, and he quickly nationalized or appropriated a number of U.S. business interests in Cuba. Many Americans feared that his brand of socialism might spread to other South American countries, just as communist insurgency had spread throughout South East Asia.

In August 1960, American President Dwight D. Eisenhower seized all Cuban assets in the United States, imposed a temporary embargo on all trade between the U.S. and Cuba, and severed diplomatic ties. In April 1961, the American government sponsored and supported an invasion of Cuba by anti-Castro exiles at the Bay of Pigs. The intention of the invasion had been to remove Castro from power, and its failure persuaded Castro that he needed the support of a major power. America clearly wasn't an option, and instead, Cuba began a relationship with the Soviet Union. Suddenly, America was faced with the worst possible situation: a country friendly to Russia only 100 miles from the shores of mainland America.

Chapter Four
The Missile Gap

"We have got to get tough with the Russians. We have got to teach them how to behave."

—President Harry S. Truman, April 1945

The year of 1960 was a presidential election year in America. Republican Dwight D. Eisenhower had served two terms as president, and his incumbent vice president, Richard Nixon, stood against Democrat John F. Kennedy. The balance of nuclear power was a major issue during the election with Kennedy claiming that the Eisenhower administration had allowed the Soviet Union to overtake America in the production of nuclear missiles. Kennedy contended that this imbalance, which came to be known as the missile gap, was dangerous, and he pledged to increase American production and deployment of ICBMs if he was elected.

The controversy about the missile gap began in 1957 with a U.S. intelligence report, which suggested that by 1965 (this was later revised to 1961) the Soviet Union might be producing as many as 500 new ICBMs each year. During the same period, it was estimated that the United States would produce around 70 new ICBMs. This, the report claimed, would lead to a dangerous gap between the number of American nuclear missiles and the number of Russian nuclear missiles. In truth, the report grossly overestimated Soviet ICBM production capacity, something that President Eisenhower knew but could not publically announce.

American Lockheed U-2 spy planes were regularly performing clandestine overflights of the Soviet Union, and these provided the president with detailed information about just how many ICBMs the Russians had. Eisenhower knew that there was indeed a missile gap, but it was in America's favor, and it would take many years for Russia to even catch up; in 1962, Russia had just 36 ICBMs compared to over 200 American ICBMs. However, Eisenhower could only announce this by admitting the existence of the U-2 program and confessing that American aircraft had been conducting illegal overflights of Soviet territory.

Due to the need to maintain the secrecy of the U-2 program, Eisenhower and Nixon were therefore unable to refute Kennedy's claim about a missile gap, even though they knew this to be untrue. When John F. Kennedy won the presidential election, he was also given access to information about Soviet ICBMs and must therefore have realized that his claims during the election had been mistaken. However, just like Eisenhower before him, he couldn't publically admit this and found himself in office on a pledge to push the production and deployment of ICBMs even though he now knew that this wasn't a military necessity.

In terms of the location of ICBMs, America already had a distinct advantage over the Soviet Union. The few Russian ICBMs were all located within the borders of the Soviet Union, far distant from targets in America. A secret CIA report produced in the early 1960s claimed that none of the Russian ICBMs had the range to reach American cities. Russia did have bombers capable of dropping nuclear bombs on the United States, but these were much easier to intercept than supersonic missiles.

The United States, however, had in 1960 and under the Eisenhower administration placed a number of Thor Intermediate Range Ballistic Missiles (IRBMs) in the United Kingdom and West Germany where they could quickly reach the main Russian cities including Moscow and Leningrad. The Thor missiles were equipped with nuclear warheads, and their placement in Europe was a source of serious concern to the Russians.

Most Americans believed in the missile gap and feared that the United States was falling behind the Soviet Union in terms of nuclear capability. This unease was reinforced when, in April 1961, Russia put the first man in space. This seemed to confirm the feeling that Soviet technology was ahead of U.S. technology and left Americans feeling even more vulnerable. This wasn't true—the Soviets placed the first man in space by ignoring potential risks while the more cautious Americans took longer because they insisted on ensuring the safety of astronauts before sending them outside the earth's atmosphere.

Despite the hysterical political rhetoric of the 1960 American presidential election, America had not fallen behind Russia in terms of nuclear weapons or technology in the early 1960s. The opposite was true—by the time that President John F. Kennedy took office in early 1961, the United States had more nuclear weapons of every type and more delivery platforms located closer to the Soviet Union. In the early 1960s, there was indeed a missile gap—but it was a gap between the Americans in the lead and the Russians lagging far behind.

Kennedy came to understand this when he took power, but he had been elected on a pledge to strengthen America's nuclear deterrent and to close what he now knew was an imaginary missile gap. Kennedy was trapped into a course of U.S. nuclear proliferation that he knew wasn't necessary or even wise.

Chapter Five

American Build-up and Provocation

"Whether you like it or not, history is on our side. We will bury you".

—Nikita Khrushchev, First Secretary of the Communist Party

When Joseph Stalin died in 1953, there was a brief power struggle in the Soviet Union to agree on a successor. Nikita Khrushchev, former head of the Communist Party in Moscow, emerged as the strongest member of the Central Committee of the Communist Party, and by 1954, he was effectively the leader of the Soviet Union. In contrast to Stalin, Khrushchev introduced reforms which were seen as liberal, including the release of many thousands of political prisoners. These proved popular with many people in the Soviet Union but also gave rise to concerns within the leadership that Khrushchev was not strong enough to be the leader of Russia.

Khrushchev responded to this with aggressive rhetoric, mainly directed at the United States and Western Europe. Then, in May 1960, the Soviet Union finally managed to shoot down one of the U-2 spy planes and captured its pilot, CIA operative Gary Powers. This was a huge embarrassment for the Eisenhower administration who had repeatedly denied that the United States operated spy aircraft over Russia, and Khrushchev used the shoot-down to attack American foreign policy.

When Democrat John F. Kennedy became president in early 1961, there was a brief improvement in U.S.-Russian relations, but this was not to last. In April 1961, President Kennedy agreed to provide limited American support for the attempted invasion of Cuba at the Bay of Pigs and the overthrow of the Castro regime by anti-Castro forces based in the United States. The invasion had been planned under the Eisenhower administration, and it was a complete failure. Cuba's ally Khrushchev and the Soviet Union responded angrily, accusing the U.S. of attacking one of Russia's main allies in the Caribbean.

In August 1961, a new political crisis erupted between the superpowers in Berlin. The German capital had been a problem since the end of World War II. Although the city was deep within the territory of East Germany, it was divided into four sectors, each ruled by one of the victorious Allied powers: America, Britain, France, and Russia. The borders within the city were notably easier to cross than other borders between East and West Germany and many people lived in one sector of Berlin but worked in another. The Russians were concerned about the number of people permanently moving from the Russian side to other sectors of the city, including numbers of prominent scientists. In response, during the early hours of Sunday, August 13, 1961, Russia suddenly sealed all borders between the Russian side and other sectors within the city. The barrier they began building on that Sunday morning would become the Berlin Wall, and for a short time, American and Russian tanks faced-off against each other on the streets of Berlin, though no shots were fired.

In late 1961, the situation worsened even further. In addition to long-range ICBMs and IRBMs, the U.S. also had shorter range nuclear-tipped missiles designed to destroy battlefield targets such as bridges and concentrations of troops and armor. The Jupiter Medium Range Ballistic Missile (MRBM) was not widely deployed within the United States, mainly because it did not have sufficient range to reach targets in the Soviet Union. Initially, the U.S. sought permission to site these missiles in France, but this was denied by French Premier Charles De Gaulle. In 1961, however, the Kennedy administration was granted permission to site Jupiter missiles with nuclear warheads in Italy and Turkey. The squadron of 15 Jupiter missiles sited in Turkey was a particular concern to the Russians—these missiles were little more than 100 miles from important Russian bases in the Black Sea which they could strike with very little warning.

Even some American politicians believed that the dispatch of Jupiter missiles to Turkey was a dangerous provocation. During a closed session of the Senate Foreign Relations Committee in 1961, Senator Albert Gore Sr. raised this issue and, in a remarkable piece of prescience, remarked to Secretary of State Dean Rusk that he "wondered what our attitude would be if the Soviets deployed nuclear missiles to Cuba?"

Documents released after the fall of the Soviet Union show that by 1961, the leaders of the Soviet Union believed that the United States was planning a decapitation nuclear strike against Russia. This belief was encouraged by the presence of Jupiter missiles in Turkey. The Jupiter missile was not protected in an underground silo as were most ICBMs. Instead, it sat in a launcher on the surface where it was very vulnerable to attack. It was therefore very unlikely that Jupiter missiles would survive to be used in a retaliatory second strike. To Soviet analysts, it seemed that the only probable use of the Jupiter was as a first-strike weapon. The location of a squadron of Jupiter missiles so close to the Russian homeland was therefore regarded as a major provocation and an act designed to destabilize the fragile nuclear balance.

In retrospect, it seems that the Soviets were probably correct. Unthinkable though it seems now, de-classified documents show that during the Berlin Crisis of 1961, the Kennedy administration did indeed give active consideration to the possibility of a first-strike nuclear attack on the Soviet Union, and the Jupiter missiles in Turkey were almost certainly intended to enhance this capability.

Russian leaders felt that it was necessary to restore the nuclear balance by placing Russian missiles an equally short distance from America. But this meant finding a country friendly to Russia which was no more than 100 miles from mainland America and which would allow the deployment of Russian missiles. It didn't take long to decide that there was only one viable location which met these requirements: the island of Cuba.

Chapter Six
Russian Missiles Arrive in Cuba

"I had the idea of installing missiles with nuclear warheads in Cuba without letting the United States find out they were there until it was too late to do anything about them."

—Nikita Khrushchev, First Secretary of the Communist Party

In February 1962, President John F. Kennedy announced that the trade embargo against Cuba was to be permanent. He also made it very difficult for American citizens to travel to Cuba and had the country expelled from the Organization of American States. Faced with a complete absence of markets in North or South America for sugar, its main export, Cuba turned to the Soviet Union for help. Russia provided Cuba with a ready market for its sugar and also sent oil, weapons, and ammunition to the island to deter an American-backed invasion.

In early 1962, Fidel Castro finally announced that he was a communist; previously he had claimed to be a Marxist and Leninist but claiming to be a communist helped cement relations between Cuba and Russia. Castro was happy to receive weapons and support from the

Soviet Union because he was afraid that the United States was plotting to remove him from power. He was right. In late 1962, President Kennedy authorized Operation Mongoose, a CIA plan to land agents on Cuba to destabilize Castro's regime and, if possible, assassinate Castro himself.

Khrushchev was keen to have more than just Russian conventional weapons located on the island, and around May 1962, the Russian premier signed off on the top-secret Operation Anadyr, a plan to covertly bring Russian nuclear missiles to Cuba and, when they were established and operational, to announce this to the world. In July, large numbers of Russian construction workers and soldiers began to arrive on Cuba. Their mission was to start building the bunkers and silos necessary for the installation of Medium Range Ballistic Missiles (MRBMs) and the bunkers required for the storage of nuclear warheads. All this was done with maximum secrecy—even the soldiers and workers brought in from Russia didn't know where they were going until they arrived on Cuba.

On August 22, 1962, the CIA received the first intelligence report from agents on the ground suggesting that there might be suspicious construction activity taking place on Cuba, though at that point there was no knowledge that this activity could be linked to nuclear weapons. The CIA ordered several U-2 overflights of the island, and on August 29, a U-2 took photographs of new Soviet anti-aircraft defenses on the island. These were SA-2 Surface-to-Air Missiles (SAM) designed to intercept high-flying aircraft, and the assumption was that the

Russian were hoping to prevent U-2 flights over the island in order to keep whatever it was they were building secret. This report also noted the presence of large numbers of Russian technicians in the Pinar del Rio province, a sparsely populated area in the west of Cuba. The report noted that all civilians had been evacuated from this area. The implication was that some large-scale secret construction activity was taking place in this region. When this was combined with a single, unconfirmed sighting by an operative on the ground of what appeared to be a Russian SS-4 MRBM being transported to the same area, there were serious concerns that the Russians might be building missile launch sites in the Pinar del Rio area.

President Kennedy sent one of his advisors to the Soviet Embassy in Washington to demand an explanation. The Russian ambassador told him that the new construction was of purely defensive structures which were being built at the request of Fidel Castro who feared another American-backed invasion. The ambassador went further—he assured the White House that Khrushchev would never site offensive weapons such as nuclear weapons on Cuba and would not do anything "to complicate the international situation or aggravate the tension in the relations between our two countries."

This put Kennedy in a very difficult situation. If the construction on Cuba was, as the ambassador claimed, purely defensive, the Americans would not be justified in taking military action to remove it. On the other hand, the presence of large numbers of Russian soldiers and construction workers on Cuba suggested that something much more significant was being built. Kennedy ordered a large number of American warships to begin training maneuvers in the Caribbean which would allow them to remain as close to Cuban water as possible. He also increased the number of photographic surveillance overflights over the island.

By the middle of September, the Americans still had no definitive proof of what the Russians were doing on Cuba, but the administration was sufficiently concerned that Kennedy gave an explicit and uncompromising warning about Cuba during a Press Conference on September 13, 1962. He spoke about the presence of Russian supplies and technicians on the island and went on to say: "If at any time the communist build-up in Cuba were to endanger or interfere with our security or if Cuba should ever become an offensive military base of significant capacity for the Soviet Union, then this country will do whatever must be done to protect its own security and that of its allies."

For the next four weeks, the Americans made concerted efforts to find out what was going on in Cuba, but bad weather prevented U-2 overflights of the island from producing useful photographic evidence. The Russians took advantage of the bad weather to accelerate progress on the construction of the missile sites. Khrushchev hoped that work on the sites would be finished before the United States became certain of what they were, and with the missiles operational, it would be too dangerous for the U.S. to take military action to have them removed.

Khrushchev later said that, by mid-October, "We hadn't had time to deliver all our shipments to Cuba, but we had installed enough missiles already to destroy New York, Chicago, and the other huge industrial cities, not to mention the little village of Washington."

On October 14, 1962, a CIA U-2 aircraft was finally able to get clear photographs of one of the Cuban construction sites in the mountains not far from the town of San Cristobal. When the photographs were analyzed by technicians at the National Photographic Interpretation Center (NPIC) they next day, were able to identify several tubes that were the same size and shape as Russian MRBMs which had been seen during the May Day Parade earlier that year. They also identified construction work consistent with launch silos to house such missiles as well as bunkers which could be used to store nuclear warheads.

The technicians at NPIC were unable to identify any nuclear warheads on the photographs, but when they were examined by experts from the CIA and the armed forces, they noted that the missile sites in the photographs could be operational in as little as two weeks. Suddenly, America was faced with the terrifying possibility of having Russian nuclear missiles less than 100 miles from the U.S. mainland.

Chapter Seven

Escalation

"We will not prematurely or unnecessarily risk the costs of worldwide nuclear war in which even the fruits of victory would be ashes in our mouth. But neither will we shrink from that risk any time it must be faced."

—President John F. Kennedy

The photographs and their interpretation by experts from the NPIC and CIA were delivered to President Kennedy on October 16, 1962 by his National Security Advisor McGeorge "Mac" Bundy. Kennedy immediately convened a meeting of the Executive Committee of the National Security Council (ExComm), a group comprising 16 of Kennedy's most trusted advisors as well as senior representatives of the State and Defense departments. Although it now seemed certain that the Russians had nuclear missiles in Cuba, it was decided that there would be no public announcement. Kennedy wanted both to avoid alarming the American public and to hide from the Russians the fact that they knew about the missiles.

Over the next five days, ExComm met regularly, and a number of additional photographs from new U-2 overflights were examined and discussed. President Kennedy attended some, but not all of these meetings. He maintained his previously agreed schedule of meetings to avoid potentially alerting the Soviets that something unusual was going on. The latest U-2 photographs confirmed that there were anything from 16 to 32 Russian missiles on Cuba. The CIA was not able to confirm the presence of nuclear warheads on the island, but it was known that the MRBMs had the range and speed to hit almost any American city within minutes of lunch from Cuba. The situation was critical, and ExComm considered four alternative responses:

1. **A negotiated response.** This would involve either open negotiation through the United Nations or secret negotiations directly with the Russians. It was felt that an offer to remove American missiles from Turkey might be required in exchange for the removal of Soviet missiles from Cuba. However, several members of ExComm were skeptical about the potential success of a negotiated response. They were concerned that this might seem like weakness on the part of America in the face of Russian aggression, and they pointed out that previous attempts to negotiate settlements with Khrushchev over the partition of Berlin had not been a success.

2. **A naval blockade of Cuba.** Secretary of Defense Robert McNamara advocated placing a U.S. Navy blockade of the island of Cuba and turning back any Soviet ships carrying equipment or supplies intended for the creation of missile sites. McNamara claimed that this would demonstrate strength and determination while avoiding armed conflict with the Soviet Union. Some members of ExComm were concerned about the legality

of such a move while others, including the president, were concerned that if the Russians already had missiles and nuclear warheads on Cuba, a blockade would simply give them more time to prepare the missiles. There was also concern that the Russians might respond with a blockade of West Berlin.

3. Air strikes. Some members of ExComm favored air strikes against the missile sites by the U.S. Air Force. Other members, however, including the president's brother, Attorney General Robert Kennedy, were concerned that this might influence international opinion against the United States. There were also doubts about the capacity of air strikes to destroy the Russian nuclear capability on Cuba—if some missiles were left intact, they might be launched against the United States in retaliation.

4. An all-out military attack on Cuba. A small number of ExComm members, led by Air Force Chief of Staff Curtis LeMay, advocated an American invasion of Cuba to capture or destroy all Soviet missiles and to remove Castro from power. LeMay even suggested a pre-emptive nuclear attack on Cuba to ensure the destruction of all Soviet nuclear missiles.

For several days, ExComm debated these alternatives. All members of the group were aware of the gravity of the situation and the importance of adopting the correct course of action. Robert Kennedy later said of these discussions, "Each one of us was being asked to make a recommendation that would affect the future of all mankind, a recommendation which, if wrong and accepted, could mean the end of the human race."

During the ExComm discussions, President John F. Kennedy had a scheduled meeting with Russian Foreign Minister Andrei Gromyko. During the meeting, Kennedy gave no clue that he knew about Russian missiles in Cuba, and he was angered when Gromyko assured him again that the construction work on Cuba was solely for the purpose of defending the Castro regime and had no offensive capability or intention.

By October 19, with President Kennedy in Chicago for a scheduled round of meetings, ExComm reduced the list of possible responses to Russia to just two options: air strikes against the missile sites or a naval blockade of Cuba. Secretary of Defense Robert McNamara remained the main advocate of a blockade, supported by Secretary of State Dean Rusk and Soviet specialist Llewellyn Thompson. Robert Kennedy was the main supporter of the air strikes option, supported by McGeorge Bundy and former Secretary of State Dean Acheson.

ExComm was deadlocked, and on October 20, President Kennedy returned to Washington from Chicago—his departure was covered by a story that he wasn't feeling well. His presence in Washington was required to break the ExComm deadlock and to decide what the American response to Russian missiles in Cuba was to be, surely one of the most difficult and potentially dangerous decisions ever faced by an American president.

Chapter Eight
Kennedy Speaks to America

"My fellow citizens: let no-one doubt that this is a dangerous and difficult effort on which we have set out. No-one can foresee precisely what course it will take or what costs or casualties will be incurred."

—President John F. Kennedy

After a great deal of deliberation, Kennedy decided to impose a naval blockade of Cuba to prevent any additional Russian supplies or technicians reaching the island. This course of action avoided a direct military confrontation with Russian forces on the island, but it was not without risk. One concern was that, if the Russians had already shipped all the necessary missiles, warheads, and construction equipment to Cuba, the blockade would not prevent the missiles from becoming fully operational. Another issue was that a blockade is considered an act of war under International Law. If the U.S. Navy established a blockade around Cuba, this could be construed as a declaration of war against an ally of the Soviet Union. Finally, if Russian ships refused to stop when ordered to do so by American warships, what would happen? If U.S. warships used their firepower to disable or destroy Russian ships in international waters, this would represent an act of war by the United States against the Soviet Union.

Despite the risks, the president decided that a naval blockade was the most effective response to Russian moves in Cuba without a direct attack on Russian armed forces known to be present on the island. On October 21, however, the administration was informed that the *New York Times* and a number of other major American newspapers had become aware of the scale and gravity of the situation in Cuba and were planning to publish articles on this subject. Wishing to avoid the possibility of panic amongst the population, President Kennedy called the editors of several newspapers and persuaded them to wait for 24 hours before publishing anything about the crisis. They all agreed, and Kennedy announced that, at seven o'clock in the evening of October 22, he would make a nationally televised speech to the American people.

Rumors of what was happening in Cuba were already circulating, and many people wondered whether the president was going to announce war with Russia. President Kennedy's televised speech was watched by more than 100 million people, and he explained that the news was grave. He noted that the Russians had placed nuclear missiles in Cuba and that this posed an unacceptable threat to the security of the United States. He called on Russia to remove the missiles and announced that the U.S. Navy would place the island of Cuba under quarantine (he was very careful to avoid the word "blockade") to prevent the arrival of any more Soviet missiles, equipment, or troops. He emphasized that humanitarian supplies, including food and medicine, would still be allowed through.

It was plain from Kennedy's speech that the outbreak of a nuclear war between Russia and America was a real possibility and that it might begin at any time. All across America, people began to construct shelters that they hoped might protect them in the event of a Russian nuclear attack. Even while the president was speaking, almost 200 U.S. Navy ships were taking up positions 800 miles from the coast of Cuba. Their orders were simple: they were to stop and search any ship approaching Cuba. Any vessel found to be carrying Soviet equipment, supplies, or personnel would be turned back. If any ship refused to stop, the Navy had orders to disable or destroy it.

The Russians reacted angrily to what they called an "act of piracy" on the part of America. In a private note sent to President Kennedy, Soviet leader Khrushchev stated: "The Soviet Government considers that the violation of the freedom to use international waters and international air space is an act of aggression which pushes mankind towards the abyss of a world nuclear-missile war." He went on to say that Russian ships would not stop if challenged by U.S. Navy vessels and that Russia would take it as an act of war if any Russian ship was fired upon by a U.S. Navy vessel.

Unknown to President Kennedy or anyone else in the American administration, there were already a number of operational Russian nuclear missiles on Cuba. Some nuclear warheads had been delivered on the freighter

Aleksandrovsk just hours before the president's speech. These weapons were protected by almost 40,000 fully armed Soviet combat troops ready to repel an American invasion and supported by jet fighter aircraft, tanks, and anti-aircraft missiles and guns. Russian ground troops also had short-range tactical nuclear weapons which were to be used to destroy any American attempt to invade Cuba.

Kennedy had given orders that ships approaching Cuba were to be stopped and searched; any ship that would not stop was to be attacked. Khrushchev had given orders that no Russian ship sailing in international waters was to stop if challenged by a U.S. Navy vessel. Two Russian freighters, the *Yuri Gagarin* and the *Kimovsk*, were known to be approaching the quarantine line and would arrive within a few days. They were supported and protected by a Russian attack submarine.

On October 22, President Kennedy raised the readiness of all U.S. armed forces to Defcon (Defense Condition) 3. Defcon 5 was the normal, peacetime state of readiness; Defcon 1 represented war. American armed forces were halfway between peace and war, and their Russian counterparts followed. The world was on the brink of an all-out war between the Soviet Union and the United States of America.

Chapter Nine
On the Edge of the Abyss

"A chain reaction will quickly start that will be very hard to stop."

—Attorney General Robert Kennedy

In the days that followed the president's television address, there was frantic discussion and negotiation. In an emergency session of the United Nations, U.S. Ambassador Adlai Stevenson presented reconnaissance photographs which showed Russian missiles on Cuba. At this point, the Soviet Union was still formally denying that there were Russian missiles on the island.

On October 26, Khrushchev sent a long, rambling, and sometimes incoherent letter directly to President Kennedy. This letter seemed to suggest that if the U.S. were to agree not to invade Cuba Russian missiles could be removed from the island. This sounded conciliatory and gave the American administration hope that the crisis could be solved by diplomacy, but in other quarters there were moves towards war.

Fidel Castro was becoming increasingly certain that the United States was about to invade Cuba and depose him. Because of this, he sent a letter to Khrushchev on October 26 in which he seemed to ask for Russia to immediately launch a pre-emptive nuclear strike against the United States. He wrote: "I believe that the imperialist's aggressiveness makes them extremely dangerous, and that if they manage to carry out an invasion of Cuba, then that would be the moment to eliminate this danger forever, in an act of the most legitimate self-defense."

On October 27, the CIA informed President Kennedy that not only were the Russian missiles on Cuba operational and ready for launch, at least some of them appeared to be armed with nuclear warheads. On the same day, Radio Moscow broadcast an aggressive speech by Khrushchev that seemed completely at odds with the moderate tone of the letter of the previous day. This speech demanded the removal of American Jupiter missiles in Turkey before Russia would consider the removal of its missiles in Cuba. Then, later the same day, another letter from Khrushchev arrived at the White House. This echoed the aggressive tone of the speech, and the members of ExComm were baffled by the very different tone of communications from Khrushchev on successive days. They assumed that he must be coming under pressure from hard-line members of the ruling group who were determined not to back down in the face of what they saw as American aggression. President Kennedy ordered U.S. armed forces to Defcon 2, the last stage of readiness before war. It would now take only a single incident to precipitate a global nuclear war.

It didn't take long for the first incident to occur. At Patrick Air Force Base in Florida, staff conducted a routine test of missile systems. When this activity was picked up by military radar further up the East Coast, it was initially mistaken for a Russian missile launch from Cuba. Fortunately, the error was identified before a retaliatory strike was launched. At Volk Air Force Base in Wisconsin, where nuclear-armed B-52 bombers were stationed, there was a brief panic when it was found that the perimeter fence had been breached. Were Russian agents on the base ready to sabotage the bombers? Fortunately, the intruder was rapidly apprehended—a large brown bear in search of food.

Other events came even closer to starting a war. Some U.S. warships which formed part of the quarantine ring around Cuba detected a group of unknown submarines in the area. They attacked but used only practice depth charges intended to force the submarines to the surface rather than destroy them. It wasn't until much later that the Americans discovered that these submarines were Russian and each was equipped with 15-kiloton nuclear torpedoes. On one of the submarines, the captain had armed a nuclear torpedo and was ready to launch it before he realized that his attackers were only using practice depth charges. He later claimed that his hand was actually over the fire-button before he realized that his submarine was not in imminent danger of destruction.

An American U-2 aircraft blundered into Russian airspace on the morning of October 27. It seems that this was a genuine mistake—the aircraft was heading for the Arctic to collect high-altitude air samples when it wandered off course. Russian interceptors were sent to investigate, and American fighters were sent to escort the U-2 back into international airspace. No shots were fired, but in the tense atmosphere of the time, it would have been understandable if the Russians had believed the U-2 to be an inbound nuclear bomber.

Then, late on October 27, Russian surface-to-air missiles were fired at another American U-2 spy plane flying a reconnaissance mission over Cuba. The U-2 was hit, and its pilot, Major Rudolph Anderson Jr., was killed. The Americans assumed that Khrushchev had authorized the SAM launch, though it later became clear that this was done by a local commander acting on his own initiative. The Joint Chiefs of Staff urged President Kennedy to immediately authorize air strikes to destroy Russian air defenses on Cuba. But Kennedy held back, realizing that any attack on Cuba might result in the launching of nuclear missiles. Instead, he sent his brother, Attorney General Robert Kennedy, to negotiate with the Soviet ambassador in the Russian Embassy in Washington during the evening of October 27.

Robert Kennedy explained that the death of Major Anderson was a major escalation in the crisis. He told the Russian ambassador, "There is now strong pressure on the president to give an order to respond with fire if fired upon. If we start to fire in response—a chain reaction will quickly start that will be very hard to stop." He also told the ambassador that America was willing to remove the Jupiter missiles from Turkey at a later date, but that it would not admit in public that this was in any way connected with the removal of Russian missiles from

Cuba. The Kennedy administration was concerned that if the U.S. was seen to remove the missiles from Turkey in response to Russian aggression it would be seen as weakness.

President Kennedy backed up the offer made by his brother with a letter to Khrushchev in which we agreed to give a guarantee that America would not invade Cuba in exchange for the removal of Russian missiles from the island. Although President Kennedy's letter did not formally agree to the removal of Jupiter missiles from Turkey, it did allude to this, noting that "easing world tensions would enable us to work towards a more general arrangement regarding other armaments."

While he awaited the Russian response, President Kennedy considered the military options available to him if negotiations should fail. American troops were stationed in Guantanamo Bay in Cuba, and from there, supported by amphibious landings, they could have started an invasion of the island as soon as the order was given. Kennedy even drafted the speech that he would give to the American people if this were to happen: "My fellow Americans, with a heavy heart I have ordered military operations with conventional weapons only to remove a major nuclear weapons build-up from the soil of Cuba."

The U.S. armed forces were confident that a combination of airstrikes and ground forces would quickly occupy Cuba and neutralize the nuclear weapons. They were completely wrong. There were not only 40,000 heavily armed Russian troops on Cuba—far more than the Americans realized—they were provided with almost 100 short-range tactical nuclear weapons which would have wiped out any invasion force.

This misunderstanding of the opposition they would face in an invasion led to American overconfidence and pressure from the Joint Chiefs of Staff on President Kennedy for military action in Cuba. From what we now know, this action would most likely have failed, and the fighting would probably have involved the use of tactical nuclear weapons which would have caused massive American casualties. It might easily have escalated into a larger scale exchange of nuclear missiles. On the night of October 27, the world held its breath as it awaited developments in the Caribbean.

Chapter Ten

The Blink

"We're eyeball to eyeball, and I think the other fellow just blinked."

—Secretary of State Dean Rusk

On the morning of October 28, 1962, President John F. Kennedy received a reply from Khrushchev. It began, "I received your message of October 27th. The Soviet Government has given a new order to dismantle the arms which you described as offensive and to crate and return them to the Soviet Union." The letter offered to carry out the dismantling and removal of all nuclear weapons on Cuba under United Nations supervision and in exchange for the end of the American quarantine of the island and a promise that no military attacks or invasion of Cuba would be undertaken by U.S. forces. In secret, the United States also agreed to the removal of all nuclear missiles in Turkey by April 1963.

Khrushchev ordered the Russian freighters heading for the quarantine line around Cuba to turn back and return the nuclear weapons they were carrying to the Soviet Union. The Cuban Missile Crisis was over, and across the world, people heaved a sigh of relief as the immediate prospect of nuclear war faded. In America, the resolution of the crisis was regarded as a victory over communist aggression. To most people, it seemed that President Kennedy had taken a strong stand and Khrushchev had been forced to back down. But not everyone was delighted with the outcome.

Fidel Castro felt betrayed by the Soviet Union because he had not been consulted before Khrushchev agreed to the removal of missiles from Cuba. He gave an angry speech in which he said: "I cannot agree with Khrushchev promising Kennedy to pull out his rockets without the slightest regard to the indispensable approval of the Cuban government." Castro was so angry that he refused to allow UN weapons inspectors on to Cuba to verify that the Russian missiles had been dismantled and were being removed. Instead, the United States was forced use overflights by reconnaissance aircraft to confirm this. This wasn't without hazard—while Khrushchev had given orders that anti-aircraft systems manned by Russian technicians were not to fire on American aircraft, those manned by Cubans still regularly tried to shoot down low-flying American aircraft. Fortunately, they didn't succeed.

President Kennedy also insisted that Russian bombers based on Cuba should be removed. These aircraft had the range to reach the United States and could potentially have been used to drop nuclear bombs. Initially, Khrushchev resisted this, but he became increasingly concerned about Fidel Castro's unpredictable and aggressive behavior, and ultimately he seemed to feel that it would be better if Russian long-range weapons were not based on Cuba. The bombers were removed, and the quarantine of Cuba was lifted. The U.S. trade embargo with Cuba, however, remained in place. The embargo forced Castro to remain an ally of Russia, and in a short time, Cuba became completely economically dependent on the Soviet Union; by the late 1980s, support for Cuba was costing the Soviet Union the equivalent of $6 billion each year.

Like Castro, many of Khrushchev's colleagues in the leadership of the Soviet Union also felt betrayed by his abrupt climb-down and saw the whole missile crisis as a mistake which reflected badly on Russia. There is no doubt that Khrushchev's intention had been to place nuclear missiles on Cuba before the United States was even aware that they existed. He then expected that Kennedy would be unable to do anything other than make bellicose speeches. He was completely taken by surprise when it appeared that the Americans were prepared to go to war over this issue. Khrushchev had no intention of entering a war that he knew the Soviet Union could not win—the missile gap in America's favor meant that any exchange of nuclear missiles would almost inevitably result in greater death and destruction in Russia than in America.

When America's determination to have the missiles on Cuba removed at all costs became clear, Khrushchev had little option but to agree. Because of the fact that the American removal of missiles from Turkey remained secret, it appeared to most outside observers that the missile crisis had ended in an embarrassing defeat for Russia. Almost precisely two years after the crisis,

Khrushchev was forced to resign as Chairman of the Council of Ministers, and his place as Soviet leader was taken by his deputy, Leonid Brezhnev. One of the main reasons for his removal was the way in which he had been seen as mishandling the Cuban Missile Crisis. Khrushchev died in retirement in 1971.

In America, President Kennedy was generally praised for his response to the crisis, and the peaceful resolution to the issue of Russian missiles in Cuba brought about the beginning of a slow change in the Cold War. Nuclear war between America and Russia no longer seemed inevitable, and in August 1963, Khrushchev and Kennedy signed the Limited Nuclear Test Ban Treaty, the first step towards limiting the proliferation of nuclear weapon testing. One other direct result of the crisis was the installation of a telephone line between the White House and the Kremlin which would allow the leaders of America and Russia to speak directly to each other if required to deal with a future crisis.

Sadly, John F. Kennedy was not allowed to see out his term of office or to completely escape repercussions of the Cuban Missile Crisis. In November 1963, just one year later, he visited the city of Dallas in Texas. Waiting for him there was Lee Harvey Oswald, a man who had served in the U.S. Marine Corps before defecting to the Soviet Union in 1959. In June 1962, he was allowed back in the United States. In America, Oswald became involved with a number of pro-Castro organizations. He developed an intense dislike of the president, in part because of his actions during the missile crisis. On November 22, 1963,

Oswald shot and killed President Kennedy as his motorcade drove through Dealey Plaza in Dallas. His brother, Robert Kennedy, who played an important role in the crisis, was also assassinated when he was campaigning for the presidential election in 1968.

Of the main players in the missile crisis, only Fidel Castro seemed unaffected. Despite many attempts to assassinate and remove him from power, he remained the president of Cuba until his retirement in 2008. He died peacefully in 2016.

Conclusion

The world has never been closer to global nuclear war than it was during two weeks in October 1962. If the United States had undertaken air strikes or an invasion of Cuba, or if a Russian submarine captain had launched a nuclear torpedo against U.S. ships, or if the U.S. Navy had attacked a Russian freighter, it is all too easy to imagine a chain-reaction spreading to conclude with the launch of ICBMs by both superpowers. In any meaningful sense, that would have precipitated the end of the world as we know it.

The fact that the crisis didn't end in nuclear war is partly a testament to the basic common-sense of two of the main protagonists: Nikita Khrushchev and John F. Kennedy. Both were aware that a nuclear war would devastate their countries and probably the entire world and both did everything they could to make sure this didn't happen. But perhaps this outcome is also a testament to the effectiveness of MAD—Mutually Assured Destruction. In a pre-nuclear age, a crisis involving Russian troops in Cuba would almost certainly have involved some level of armed conflict. But at a time when war meant almost certain destruction for everyone involved, no-one could afford to let fighting supplant negotiating.

In that sense, the Cuban Missile Crisis exemplifies the Cold War between America and Russia. Both sides constantly maneuvered to gain the best advantage but, when confronted by a resolute defense, neither could afford to allow the situation to escalate to all-out war.

Printed in the USA
CPSIA information can be obtained
at www.ICGtesting.com
LVHW020257301024
795202LV00002B/275

The Cold War between the United States of America and the Soviet Union lasted for more than 40 years. In general, this was a war of spies and subterfuge, of covert action and espionage. There was always a danger, however, that an error of judgment on either side could suddenly cause the Cold War to turn red-hot with an exchange of nuclear weapons. On many occasions, tensions between the countries increased, but the prospect of all-out nuclear war between America and Russia was never closer than during a two-week period in October of 1962.

In response to the placement of American nuclear missiles in Turkey, Soviet leader Nikita Khrushchev secretly ordered the transport of Russian nuclear missiles to the island of Cuba in the Caribbean. These were capable of reaching and destroying almost all American cities in a matter of minutes. When this was discovered, the U.S. administration under President John F. Kennedy decided that the threat had to be removed, even if this meant risking war with Russia. The Americans set up a blockade of the island and considered air strikes and even a full-scale invasion of Cuba. Forty thousand heavily armed Russian and Cuban troops supported by tanks, aircraft, and even tactical nuclear weapons stood by to do anything required to repel an American attack.

ISBN 9781721659869

THE CUBAN MISSILE CRISIS
A History From Beginning to End